100 Social Tips for English

With a very short history of English

G.J.Hutt

Exposure Publishing

100 Social Tips for English

First published in Great Britain 2006 by

Exposure Publishing, an imprint of Diggory Press,
Three Rivers, Minions, Liskeard, Cornwall, PL14 5LE, UK
WWW.DIGGORYPRESS.COM

British Library Cataloguing In Publication Data
A Record of this Publication is available
from the British Library

ISBN 1846852609
978-1-84685-260-2

100 Social Tips for English

100 Social Tips for English

How to succeed and have smooth conversations
with more fun when dealing with English speakers

- it's the little things that matter -

English social life is very flexible and there no real rules
that you have to follow.

This is sometimes a reason for foreigners
feeling uncomfortable in English groups –
they would rather have some concrete rules.

The English notice that something is wrong and
they feel that they are not doing the right thing.

So, just relax.

Don't feel uncomfortable about your use of English. The
English make no judgements about how good or bad
your English is – as long as they understand what you
are saying.

Never be afraid to say 'I don't understand' or 'I don't
follow' –
we use these phrases a lot as a kind of ploy. Nobody
minds explaining.

Taking part in discussions and conversations is the only
important thing –

and these tips show you how to do it.

Contents

Tip 1

In English social life there are no hard and fast rules. Not everybody stands up when you enter a room or join a group, for example. Whether they do or don't, has no meaning.

Because our social behaviour is very flexible, you should never let this make you feel uncomfortable.

Tip 2

In English, hand-shaking is really optional when meeting people. It happens more in business transactions than in social life.

If the English forget to shake hands when you think they should, it doesn't have any meaning.

Tip 3

In English, we always use the first name in nearly all situations. Again, this has no meaning – it's just normal – you can't interpret anything into the use of the first name.

If this is unfamiliar to you, introduce yourself using both names. This applies to both men and women.

Tip 4

Being introduced formally is not something that always happens in English social life. Again, there are no hard and fast rules.

We often begin talking to people without knowing who they are. We find that out later.

Tip 5

In conversations and discussions you have to keep responding to what is being said otherwise the English stop speaking.

You keep responding by saying things like 'oh yes' 'I see'. Giving some gesture like nodding is also useful.

Tip 6

In conversations and discussions when you are speaking allow a pause for English speakers to respond.

This can sometimes seem that the English speakers are trying to interrupt. This isn't so – it is just our normal need for inter-action.

Tip 7

You can speak to people without having been introduced. This applies to both men and women.

This is quite normal in English. At a suitable point you can then introduce yourself to the other person.

Tip 8

Always be willing to start and respond in conversations and discussions. There is no order or rank in English.

Listen to English speakers and notice how this happens all the time.

Tip 9

Asking questions and listening to answers is a very good way of starting conversations.

Tip 10

Notice and comment on any pet animals – many English speakers prefer them to people.

Tip 11

Assume conditions are perfect ..

.. even if they aren't.

Tip 12

Try never to refuse a cup of tea ..

But you don't have to drink it. Tea is partly an invitation to talk as much as a drink.

Tip 13

*Avoid using the words 'yes' and 'no' too much.
They can sound very confronting in English.*

Tip 14

Be interested rather than interesting.

Tip 15

Try to make others ask you what you want to say.

We say something out of context to get the response 'I don't follow' or 'I don't understand' - then we go ahead.

Tip 16

At a set meal you can start eating without saying anything.

We don't say things like 'good appetite'.

Tip 17

Start drinking without saying anything.

Tip 18

Never criticise food and drink.

Tip 19

Avoid comparisons with your own culture.

Tip 20

If you like someone of the opposite sex let them know indirectly.

Tip 21

Avoid the use of all titles on social occasions.

Tip 22

Modify what you disagree with without disagreeing.

Tip 23

Always be willing to stop talking and listen.

Tip 24

Try to avoid excessive gestures.

Tip 25

Try to avoid excessive compliments.

Tip 26

Try to avoid too much touching.

Tip 27

In English, conversations and discussions move forward point by point NOT person by person.

Tip 28

Because it is very easy to be forceful, aggressive and insulting in English – just by leaving out signals – there are not so many violent gestures needed.

Tip 29

Never over-complicate what you have to say with too many words.

Tip 30

Question for information without pressing for it.

Tip 31

Assume others know what you want to say.

Tip 32

Don't ask for unreasonable promises or commitment.

Tip 33

Accept and modify indirect agreement.

Tip 34

Don't argue further after agreement has been reached.

Tip 35

Beware of sentences spoken in the conditional tenses.

They can sound like agreement but mean the opposite.

Tip 36

Beware of the word 'yes'.

It mostly means 'carry on talking'.

Tip 37

Use conditional tenses when talking about possible risks and dangers.

Tip 38

Always assume agreement can be reached.

Tip 39

Never begin by assuming something is impossible.

Tip 40

Make sure you listen to everyone's opinion.

Tip 41

Always leave the door open for future negotiation.

Tip 42

Avoid personal attacks on others.

Tip 43

The correct way to address the Monarch in public
is –
Your Majesty

Tip 44

The correct way to address a first prince or
princess in public is -

Tip 45

The correct way to address a High Court Judge in public is -

Tip 46

The correct way to address a Mayor or Magistrate in public is -

Tip 47

The correct way to address an Arch-bishop in public is -

Your Eminence.

Tip 48

The correct way to address a person with the title 'Sir' in public is to join the 'Sir' to the first name -

'Sir John Brown' is 'Sir John' - *never* 'Sir Brown'.

Tip 49

On formal introductions we use the greeting 'How do you do?' The reply is the same.

Tip 50

You can only use this formal introduction once with the same person. Using it on a subsequent occasion would imply that you had forgotten who that person was.

Tip 51

The words 'Sir' and 'Madam' mean something like 'valued customer'.

Tip 52

'Mr' 'Mrs' and 'Miss' identify a persons' function.

Tip 53

The English form queues when waiting for buses or in shops when waiting to pay. It is almost an art form, often with elaborate systems to help this happen.

Tip 54

Never obviously push through a group. Gently ease your way firmly forward.

Tip 55

English traffic regulations and road signs are fairly international and are relatively easy to follow.

Tip 56

Be kind to animals in public.

Tip 57

Avoid drunk football fans at all times.

Tip 58

Make complaints quietly.

Tip 59

Choose foreign restaurants.

Tip 60

Don't touch strange women/men in public places.

Tip 61

In pubs you pay for each drink at the bar. There is no service for drinks.

Tip 62

We still order in pints and in halves – but the measure is metric.

You say 'A pint of ..' or 'A half of ..' and then add the name of the beer or the type.

.. wine is ordered as red or white.

Tip 63

We usually order whisky by the distillery name. If you want a large one you ask for a 'double'.

Tip 64

On the road, don't shout loudly at other drivers or pedestrians.

Tip 65

When driving, avoid loud and long hooting in traffic.

Don't ask for jokes to be explained.

Tip 67

Laugh politely at jokes and remarks you don't understand.

Tip 68

Don't discuss bodily functions.

Tip 69

Don't dance, sing or undress in the street.

Don't call Scotsmen English.

Tip 71

Don't tell an English person that they have no sense of humour.

Tip 72

When a person says 'Thank you.' that's the end of the conversation.

Tip 73

With a group drinking in a pub, we buy 'rounds' for the group.

Tip 74

When paying in a restaurant don't shout loudly for the waiter.

Tip 75

We give tips to taxi drivers.

Tip 76

We give tips to waiters.

Tip 77

We give tips to porters.

Tip 78

We give tips to restaurant and hotel Doormen.

Tip 79

We give tips to Messengers and Delivery Operatives.

Tip 80

We don't give tips to Barmen in pubs, they refuse to take them – occasionally from foreigners.

Tip 81

Take a cue from those around you – don't dress ostentatiously in public.

Tip 82

You can dress outrageously.

Tip 83

Here are some phrases for offering things.

Tip 84

Never say 'no' – except on special occasions –
unless you want to cause friction.

Tip 85

*Never say 'no' – except on special occasions –
unless you want to cause friction.*

Tip 86

Never say 'no' – except on special occasions –
unless you want to cause friction.

Tip 87

Never say 'no' – except on special occasions –
unless you want to cause friction.

Tip 88

*Never say 'no' – except on special occasions –
unless you want to cause friction.*

Tip 89

Some ways of asking people to do things - 'Would you mind …. ing?'

Some ways of asking people to do things - 'Do you think you could ….?'

Tip 91

Some ways of asking people to do things - 'Do you mind if ....?'

Tip 92

Some ways of asking people to do things - 'I'm afraid I must ask you to ….'

Tip 93

In most other cultures Overstatements are positive
– in English it is the opposite -

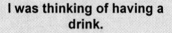

I was thinking of having a drink.

Overstatement

It can only be your incredible beauty that has so confused me that I am unable to decide even the simplest thing for myself, so please understand that I need your help to decide. The moment that you speak a new era will begin, so if you say 'no' there will be no further discussion. On that basis will you have a drink with me?

Because English verb grammar can be quite complicated, both those statements mean the same thing.

Tip 94

Understatement

Tip 95

Understatement

It's a pretty sunset, isn't it?

Overstatement

This reminds me of those high slopes in the Andes where the sunsets are as equally brilliant in colour and atmosphere, the vivid hues and change in nuance is as rare a phenomenon as I have ever seen in the northern hemisphere.

Understatement

The English accept and adapt to conversations with foreigners.

Tip 98

Up to a point the English have no concept of good or bad or unacceptable language and they don't make these judgements.

Tip 99

As long as what you say is understandable it is perfectly acceptable.

Fort Morgan Library & Musuem Services
970-542-4000
www.cityoffortmorgan.com

Customer ID: A9/953052163
Circulation system messages:
Patron status is ok.

Title: 100 social tips for English : with a very
short history of English
ID: U190201266318
Due: 03/12/2013 23:59:59
Circulation system messages:
Item checkout ok.

Total items: 1
2/19/2013 10:04 AM

Circulation system messages:
End Patron Session is successful

Thank you for using the
3M SelfCheck™ System.

Tip 100

A Very Short History of the English Language

Ancient language
Circa 2500BC - 57AD

It is difficult to be definite about the ancient history of the English language. What can be said is that it is one of what are called the Low German dialects - this has nothing to do with what is now modern German.

Presumably, when the British Isles were still attached to the mainland of northern Europe, the various tribes in that area spoke dialects of a similar root language. When the British Isles separated from the mainland the people on the islands developed in a different way from the cultures that they had left behind. None-the-less there are traces in Old English of the roots of the dialects that existed in North Western Germany, Denmark, the Friesen Islands and the Netherlands.

Little is known of the Island language. In common with many other cultures of the period, it was not written down from its origins. Although it was a sophisticated culture - for the time - there is very little evidence available. The oldest man-made structure in Western Europe is Stonehenge in Southern England which dates from around 3000-4000BC. There are legends that were handed down by word of mouth and recorded at later dates. There are artefacts and archaeological remains that show there were complex spiritual rituals and the like, much the same as happened in North Western Europe, but, of course, having developed differently.

The ancient Phoenicians visited the island - presumably to trade - and there was contact with other civilizations.

So, for some 3000 years before the birth of Christ, the people, the culture and the language were developing along the same lines as North Western European societies but in isolation from them. The Nordic and Germanic myths and legends are very similar in context and feeling to those that were handed down in Britain.

57AD - 410AD The Roman Invasion

In 55AD the first Roman invasion of Britain took place. It failed and the Romans were defeated. They returned two years later with a much larger force and, in spite of the resistance and fierce battles, the English lost and Britain became part of the Roman Empire.

This was very significant in the development of English. The official language of the country became Latin and the infra-structure of the country expanded rapidly under Roman rule. English does not appear in any of the documents of the period and all positions of power were taken over by Roman officials.

English became a spoken language used by what the Romans regarded as an under-class.

From constant contact with rulers and administrators, through working and socializing, the two communities came closer together. Many Latin words entered the English language. They got modified and were used by the general population in their daily lives.

There was inter-marriage between the two communities and English developed an ever increasing stock of new words transformed from Latin and anglicized. But English remained a second class language and all teaching and learning was done in Latin. During this period Britain became Christianized. All the sites of Pagan worship were demolished and churches were built.

45 - 1150 Old English Period

When the Romans left England about 410AD there was a vast legacy of roads and civil engineering works left behind, not to mention a mixed population, but more importantly, the development of the English language during the occupation had been immense.

After the departure of the Romans English began to re-establish itself and develop further, however, the language of the church and learning - as well as much administration - remained in Latin. In spite of this, some important works were produced in English, notably by the Venerable Bede, a monk in northern England. His books are thought to be the first scholarly works written in English.

749 The Angles Invasion

The first change in this pattern, at around 749AD, was the invasion of Southern England by the Angles and the Jutes from the area that is now North Germany and Denmark.

There was some resistance and some battles between the factions but Angles and Jutes took over and the indigenous population moved away to the west and the north. However, after a period of time, through trade, work, expansion, cooperation and inter-marriage between the more powerful families and the population as a whole, there ceased to be a difference between the tribes and there was the beginning of the foundation of a nation. Under King Harold the country became more unified and learning and scholarship was encouraged as the language developed with the new concepts that were being discovered.

The difference in the languages was diminished by the exchange of words into one and the other until this eventually became unified as Old English. It must be remembered that Old English has very little to do with modern English. As with most modern languages, the old version is unintelligible unless it is learned like a foreign language.

The Viking Invasion

During this Old English period the Vikings, from what is now northern Scandinavia, started raiding northern England. At some point they occupied parts of the North East of the country. There were battles and victories and defeats on both sides, but many Vikings settled in the north. They farmed and built alongside the native population.

Again the two cultures came together and, over time, merged into one. The Old English of the time absorbed more words and became, itself, modified by the Norse.

However, King Harold did not want the north of the country to be colonized by the Vikings, so many battles were fought, lost and won.

While King Harold was fighting the Vikings in the North - a battle which he convincingly won - another unexpected event occurred in the South.

1066 The Norman Invasion

It needs to be understood that, in 1066, that part of Northern France that is now Normandy, was, at this time, a Viking colony. This colony had been set up several hundred years before with the support of the King of France. 'Norman' means 'North-man' in the language of the time.

In a relatively short space of time, the Vikings adopted the French language - this was as different from modern French as old English is different from the modern language - and Norman-French was different again. The Normans had added greatly to the prosperity and development of France as a whole.

There had been contact and some inter-marriage among the English and Norman Royalty, but in 1066 the Norman King, William, decided to invade England. There was a fierce battle on the South Coast. The Anglo-Saxon King Harold had hurried from the North, after fighting the Vikings, to the battle with a depleted army. He was killed and the Norman Conquest had begun. William was crowned King of England on Christmas Day of 1066.

William disinherited and disfranchised all Anglo-Saxon nobles and aristocrats, and a great many were murdered and executed. The church leaders and administrators were replaced by Normans. The language of the administration was Norman-French. Prayer, teaching and officialdom were in Latin or Norman-French. Every possible position of power in the country was in the hands of Normans brought to England to achieve the objective of the domination of Britain.

English, for next two hundred or so years, was reduced to a second class language spoken by what the Normans regarded as an under class.

English remained the language of the people - but there are still fine examples of literature from this period of English. After time, the same thing happened as with the Romans before. Close contact, economy, inter-marriage, the development and expansion of the infra-structure, expanding population and the need to instil the fear of God into the people all led to English absorbing and anglicizing a large number of Norman words into the daily use of the Old English language.

Many of the Norman nobles in England had large estates and lands in France. For political reasons the King of France decided that Normans would have to decide whether to keep their lands in England or in France - but not both. Many returned to France, but many others were, by then, so integrated into the culture that had developed in England that they stayed and were absorbed into the ever growing Anglo-Saxon society.

1150 - 1500 Middle English

After 1220 or so begins the time of the reinstatement of English - this lasted until around 1500. This was a gradual process at first with many teachers and scholars still working in Latin, but, with the clergy anxious to spread the word of God to as many people as possible, gradually English started to be used. Slowly English was used more and more for administrative and legal matters. Many books were translated and as a result new words were taken over into English.

This process went on relentlessly, in spite of those of the establishment who wanted to retain Latin as the basis of all learning. However, in the end, this had little impact and in 1425 English was declared the official language of the Court and of the Administration of the country. Toward the end of this period Thomas Caxton brought printing to England. This changed a great many things. As far as the language is concerned it brought about the need for standardization.

There were five major dialects in the country. It must be pointed out that a dialect is a language within a language - but it is a language in its own right. It is therefore not intelligible to those of other dialects. This is not the same as an 'accent'. An accent is a different way of making a sound. In modern English there are no real dialects that are spoken now, but there are many accents. However, in the Middle English period there were five dialects. A book published in one dialect would be unintelligible to the others.

1500 The Modern Period

Given that the political system and the church were keen to reach as many people as possible, the book provided the ideal way of doing this and it was decided by the Royal Society to use the London dialect. This duly happened, so, over several generations, this was the standard that English would take. This does not mean that everybody sounded the same - but it did mean that they were speaking the same language.

The advent of printing saw floods of books being written and translated and, all the time, the ideas and the vocabulary were absorbed into English and were being used by the people. There was an explosion of ideas and new worlds were on the verge of being discovered. At this point, the English vocabulary in use was some three times greater than comparable languages of the period. Where one concept had three words, each one had - and still has - subtle differences in meaning.

This tool of English gave vast scope for human expression and at the end of this period had given rise to Geoffrey Chaucer and William Shakespeare as well as many other writers and scholars. Discoveries from the new worlds that had been found brought new words to add to the language. English was being modernized all the time.

Up to this period and throughout its known history English had developed without restrictions. During the Roman Invasion, the Viking Invasion, the Angles invasion, the Norman invasion and subsequent occupation and subjugation of the English, the language was only used by the people - the ruling classes left the language to its own devices. There was no scholarship in English, no rules of grammar as such, no authority to say what was right or wrong. The people developed it themselves through usage. It was this random process that had led English to this unique position. English spelling is one of the results of this personalization and of not having had any rules.

By this time French and Italian had been formalized, grammar documented and an authority imposed on them, rigorously backed up by the Roman Catholic Church.

English was still wild, ungoverned, unregulated, varying from one person to another, each of whom could make what changes were felt necessary to express an idea.

There was, of course, a grammar and rules of word order - but nobody had ever written them down or thought about them. Due to its history English was only inside the heads of those who spoke it.

It is this chaotic, ill-defined and unregulated language that provided the tool to produce some of the greatest literature in history.

Toward the end of this period England began exploring and discovering new worlds and territories - the first steps to the building of the empire. This again had an impact on the language. With each discovery came the need express new concepts - often using borrowed words from the native tongues.

At the beginning this period there was a change of attitude. It was not until 1664 that the English scholar, Dryden, realized that there was no formulated version of what English should be like. He, and some others, proposed that there should be an English Academy to regulate and fix the English language. The French and Italians had already set these up even a hundred years before this.

In general this idea was rejected on the grounds that a living language cannot be regulated and fixed for all time. In any case, the purpose of the French and Italian academies was not proving successful. English was left to develop in its own way.

There was not - and never has been - an institution to dictate what English should be like.

It was agreed that a dictionary was needed as not all English speakers gave the same meaning to the same word.

This work was done by an individual, Samuel Johnson, who, in 1755, publish his dictionary after working seven years, almost alone, to compile it. It was not perfect - but it was there.

Grammar was different. Many attempts were made to formulate an English Grammar, but none of them succeeded. Many scholars made the mistake of trying to equate English grammar with Latin. It was eventually realized that the English grammar model did not fit into Latin.

For much of its history English was only spoken by a subjugated people - now Anglo-Saxons. During the course of its development through use it had become simplified. Any artificial element, and any element that did not serve the purpose of direct communication, was removed. English noun grammar is the simplest of all modern languages - and, partly, does conform to the Latin pattern. English verb grammar does not and cannot. The reasons are given later.

The 19th and 20th Centuries

The growth of science and industrialization had the biggest affect on the language during this period. The lack of restrictions and formulations in English makes it very easy to invent a new word in a variety of ways, the only condition being 'that it sounds right'.

It is clear that a great many other events took place, the expansion of the British Empire, wars, naval power and the control of commercial trade, all had their influence on the world - but not so much on the English language. There were changes, but these were mostly to do with social status and the divisions of the classes rather than any fundamental influence, and such influences are usually a matter of fashion in a language. What is right today maybe wrong tomorrow.

In the colonies no official effort was made to teach the people English or to stop them speaking their own language. Rather like the Romans, the English remained largely indifferent to the cultures they had subdued - there are many notable exceptions of course. Any English teaching was carried out by missionaries anxious to convert the people to Christianity.

At the end of the 19th century the British Empire covered two thirds of the globe, so, in order to do business and survive, you needed to speak English - even to start a revolt against them. It is easy to see why and how English has spread.

The 20th century has helped this spread through many ways. The growth of America, the Commonwealth Countries, the globalization of industry, the media, travel and many other forms of inter-action. Now we have the new forms of electronic communication and the internet, there are even more possibilities.

English is used in many other countries in a form that has been developed by the people who live there - and this will continue into the future.

The English Language has a unique history. It has been left - and is still left - to look after itself. It develops in its own way, moulded by the people who speak it. It has not been fettered by restrictions and prescriptions of an elite group of scholars. Certain groups did - an occasionally still do - try to restrict the use of English, but nobody takes any notice.

Apart from the obvious political, industrial and historical events that have put English into this 'world class' there are features of the language itself that have helped bring this about.

For reasons already explained, the noun grammar of English has been reduced to the minimum - anything superfluous or artificial has been removed over the course of its history and the only elements that actually have true meaning remain.

Its long history of freedom from restriction allows speakers to add new concepts and modifications to express ideas - without the fear of being labelled 'inferior' in their knowledge of the language.

The most different feature in English is the verb grammar. This is probably based on a Celtic model that has only survived because it has never been made to conform to Latin. The difference can be said to be that Latin grammar is 'internal' in that it requires the speaker to take up a point of view with regard to the relationship between the words of the sentence to be formed - and also to the person being addressed - as these things condition the grammar to be used. In addition the form of that grammar is fixed. The Celtic model requires the speaker to take up an 'external' view in that the position in time and the external causes of the event dictate the grammar. The grammar is not fixed because the model provides only half the grammar needed - the other half is selected by the speaker at that given moment.

This sounds complicated, but once you know the model it becomes an instinct. You can put small foreign children into a group of English children and within a short space of time the foreigners will become English speakers without knowing how or why. Adults, on the other hand, approach the language analytically - from their own model's point of view - and consequently take longer to learn. The new verb grammar is the subject of the book 'The Hidden Meaning in English Sentence Structure' and the CD Roms 'The Vital English Verb System'.

The rhetoric of the language has evolved on democratic principles which enables - at least in word - that everyone is equal. Probably because of having been subjugated for such a long period by conquerors, Anglo-Saxons developed a different way of dealing with others. The behaviour is non-confrontational - until confrontation is needed. This is the subject of the book 'The Code and Guidelines of Anglo-Saxon Communication' and the CD Rom 'English Language Rhetoric for Everyday Use'.

A further difference that has developed in English is that the sounds that make up the language are put together in way unlike most other languages. English does not have the sound-concept of equal stress and equal length of syllables. These features are the subject of the book 'The Sounds that Make English' and the CD Rom 'The Sounds of Fluent English'.

This development process in the English language will go on and continue developing in unknown ways as more people around the world use it.

English has never needed purists, grammarians and linguists to tell it what to do - it just needs people to speak it.

Printed in the United States
80158LV00002B/3